ANIMALS

Frogs

by Kevin J. Holmes

Content Consultant:
Rafe M. Brown
Department of Zoology and
Texas Memorial Museum
University of Texas

Bridgestone Books
an imprint of Capstone Press

Bridgestone Books are published by Capstone Press
818 North Willow Street, Mankato, Minnesota 56001
http://www.capstone-press.com

Library of Congress Cataloging-in-Publication Data
Holmes, Kevin J.
   Frogs/by Kevin J. Holmes.
   p. cm.--(Animals)
   Includes bibliographical references (p. 23) and index.
   Summary: An introduction to frogs' physical characteristics, habits, prey, and relationships
to humans.
   ISBN 1-56065-745-6
   1. Frogs--Juvenile literature. [1. Frogs.] I. Title. II. Series: Holmes, Kevin J.   Animals.
QL668.E2H78   1998
597.8'9-dc21

                                          97-31853
                                             CIP
                                             AC

Editorial credits:
Editor, Martha E. Hillman; cover design, Timothy Halldin; photo research, Michelle L. Norstad

Photo credits:
Dembinsky Photo Assoc. Inc./John Mielcarek, 10; Skip Moody, 12, 18; Gary
   Meszaros, 14
Root Resources/Anthony Merciena, 4
John G. Shedd Aquarium, 6
Michael P. Turco, cover, 8
Unicorn Stock Photos/Ted Rose, 16; B. W. Hoffmann, 20

Table of Contents

Eyes

Mouth

Legs

Fast Facts

Kinds: There are more than 4,100 kinds of frogs.

Range: Frogs live everywhere in the world except Antarctica.

Habitat: Most frogs live near ponds, lakes, and rivers. Some live in trees in rain forests. Some live under the ground in deserts.

Food: Frogs eat insects, worms, small fish, slugs, and other small animals.

Mating: Most frogs mate in the spring. Some frogs can mate at any time.

Young: Most frogs are tadpoles before they are adult frogs. Tadpoles hatch from eggs. They change into adult frogs.

Frogs

Frogs are amphibians. An amphibian is a cold-blooded animal with a backbone. Cold-blooded means having body heat that changes with the outside weather. The animal's body heats up in warm weather. Its body cools off in cold weather.

Frogs move between warm and cold places. This keeps them from becoming too warm or too cold.

Most young amphibians live in water. Most adults live on land. But adult amphibians often live near the water.

There are more than 4,100 kinds of frogs in the world. They live everywhere except Antarctica. About 100 kinds of frogs live in North America.

Most frogs live a few years. Flat-headed frogs live in the deserts of Australia. These frogs live as long as 10 years.

There are more than 4,100 kinds of frogs in the world.

Appearance

Frogs are many colors. Frogs can be green, brown, red, yellow, blue, or black. Many frogs are more than one color. Some frogs have clear skin. They are called glass frogs.

Frogs are many sizes. Some frogs are as small as one-half inch (1.3 centimeters) long. The largest frogs are Goliath frogs. They can be more than two feet (61 centimeters) long.

Frogs have different body features. They can have large or small eyes. Some have eyes on top of their heads. Some have eyes on the sides of their heads. Frogs can have wide or narrow mouths. Their skin is usually wet.

All frogs have four legs. Their back legs are longer than their front legs. Their back legs are strong. They help frogs swim and hop. Some frogs can hop 20 times their body length. Some frogs have webbed feet. Their toes are connected by skin. Webbed feet help frogs swim.

Frogs are many colors.

Homes

Most frogs must live near water to keep their skin wet. Sometimes frogs use their skin to breathe. To do this, their skin must be wet. Their skin takes in oxygen from the water. Their skin also takes in water. Frogs do not need to drink water through their mouths.

Many frogs live near ponds or marshes. A marsh is an area of low, wet land. Some frogs live near lakes or rivers. Tree frogs live in trees. They live in rain forests in South America and Asia. Some frogs live underground in deserts. They live in North America, South America, and Africa.

Some frogs estivate during dry or hot periods. Estivate means to spend time in a deep sleep. Frogs dig holes and cover themselves. They estivate until rain falls or the air cools.

Other frogs hibernate. Hibernate means to spend the winter in a deep sleep. These frogs also dig holes. They wake up in spring.

Most frogs must live near water to keep their skin wet.

Mating

Frogs mate in spring. Mate means to join together to produce young. Frogs use croaking sounds to call to mates. Each kind of frog makes different croaking noises.

Some male frogs fight for females. They may fight for hours. The male that wins the fight mates with the female.

Male frogs climb onto the backs of females to mate. They hold on to the females with their front arms. After mating, males try to find another mate.

Female frogs can lay between 100 and 20,000 eggs each year. Frogs usually lay eggs in the water. The eggs often float on the surface.

Some frogs care for their eggs. They carry the eggs on their backs. These frogs put the eggs in water when the tadpoles are ready to hatch.

Frogs use croaking sounds to call mates.

Life Stages

Most frogs go through three life stages. They begin as eggs. The eggs have soft, clear shells. A jelly covers them. It keeps the eggs warm.

Tadpoles hatch from eggs. They have tails and large heads. Tadpoles eat most of the time. They breathe through gills on their skin. A gill is an organ on a tadpole's side that helps it breathe. The gills take in oxygen from the water.

Tadpoles usually change slowly. First, they grow legs. Then tadpoles grow lungs. Their gills become smaller and disappear. Finally, tadpoles lose their tails. Tadpoles are then adult frogs.

Some kinds of frogs become adults in a few months. Other kinds take up to two years to become adults.

Some frogs do not go through these life stages. They are never tadpoles. They are young adult frogs when they hatch from eggs.

Tadpoles have tails and large heads.

Food

Frogs eat different foods during each life stage. Tadpoles eat small water plants and animals.

Adult frogs are predators. A predator is an animal that hunts other animals for food. Adult frogs eat bugs, worms, and slugs. They also eat small fish and mice.

Frogs catch prey with their long, sticky tongues. Prey is an animal hunted by another animal for food. Frogs' tongues connect near the front of their mouths. This helps them flip their tongues out quickly to catch prey.

Most frogs swallow prey without chewing. They stuff large prey into their mouths with their front feet.

Frogs also use their eyes for swallowing. Their eyes sit above their throats. They pull their eyes inside their heads. Their eyes are so large that they push prey down frogs' throats.

Frogs catch prey with their tongues.

Enemies

Frogs have different enemies during each life stage. Fish, turtles, water insects, and birds eat frog eggs.

Salamanders, snakes, and fish eat tadpoles. Many tadpoles stay safe by hiding. Camouflage also keeps tadpoles safe. Camouflage is coloring that makes an animal look like its surroundings. Predators often cannot see the tadpoles.

Birds, turtles, and snakes eat frogs. Otters, skunks, and fish also eat frogs. Frogs can usually stay safe. They can hear and see predators. They can jump away quickly.

Camouflage keeps many frogs safe. Some frogs can change their colors to match their surroundings.

Brightly colored frogs like poison dart frogs are often poisonous. Their bright colors warn predators not to eat them. Animals that eat these frogs might become sick or die.

Frogs have different enemies during each life stage.

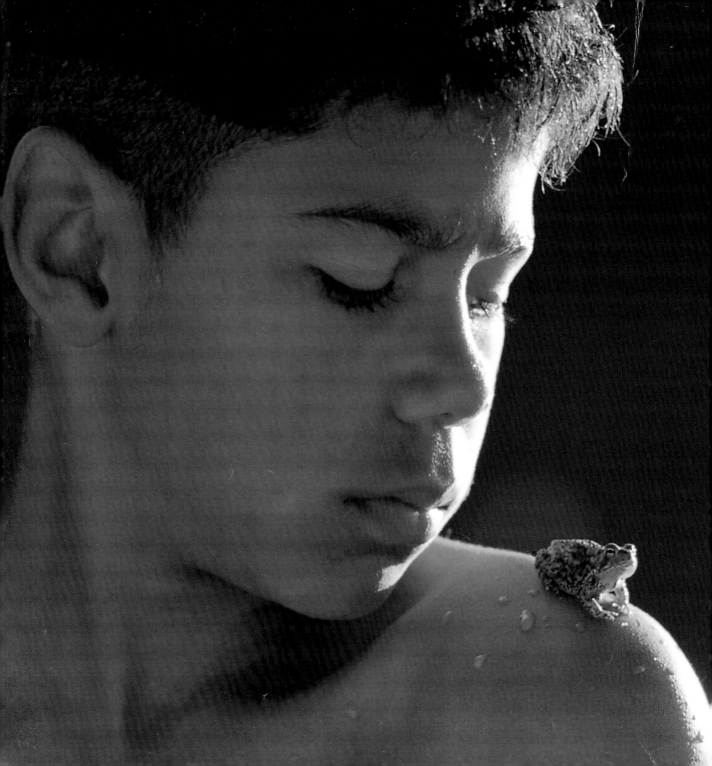

Frogs and People

Frogs help people by eating insects. Some insects spread illness to people. Other insects eat people's crops.

Scientists use the poison from poison dart frogs to make drugs. These drugs help stop pain.

Sometimes people hurt frogs. Some people destroy rain forests, ponds, and marshes where frogs live. This means frogs have fewer places to live. Many kinds of frogs are now extinct. Extinct means no longer living anywhere in the world.

Some people put poisons on their lawns and crops to kill insects. Sometimes these poisons wash into ponds, rivers, and marshes. The poisons hurt frogs.

People can keep water cleaner by using less poison. They can help save areas where frogs live. This will keep frogs and their homes safe.

People can help save areas where frogs live.

Hands On: Frog Race

Frogs leap from place to place. They jump away from predators. You can leap like a frog.

What You Need

A large playing area
Two or more players

What You Do

1. Choose a starting line and a finish line.
2. All players should bend their knees. They should put their hands on the ground in front of them. This is the frog position. Practice leaping like a frog.
3. Line up along the starting line in frog position.
4. Pick one person to say go.
5. All players should leap to the finish line.
6. The first player to reach the finish line wins.

Words to Know

amphibian (am-FIB-ee-uhn)—a cold-blooded animal with a backbone

camouflage (KAM-uh-flahzh)—coloring that makes an animal look like its surroundings

cold-blooded (KOHLD-BLUHD-id)—having body heat that changes with the outside weather

estivate (ES-tuh-vate)—to spend time in a deep sleep during dry or hot periods

hibernate (HYE-bur-nate)—to spend the winter in a deep sleep

mate (MATE)—to join together to produce young

predator (PRED-uh-tur)—an animal that hunts other animals for food

prey (PRAY)—an animal hunted by another animal for food

Read More

Pascoe, Elaine. *Tadpoles*. Woodbridge, Conn.: Blackbirch Press, 1997.

Patent, Dorothy Hinshaw. *Flashy Fantastic Rain Forest Frogs*. New York: Walker and Company, 1997.

Useful Addresses

Center for Global
  Environmental Education
1536 Hewitt Avenue
St. Paul, MN 55104-1284

Center for North American
  Amphibians and Reptiles
1502 Medinah Circle
Lawrence, Kansas 66047

Internet Sites

The Frog Page
http://www.geocities.com/TheTropics/1337/index.html
Froggy Page
http://frog.simplenet.com/froggy/
The Somewhat Amusing World of Frogs
http://www.csu.edu.au/faculty/commerce/account/
  frogs/frog.htm

Index